UNION PACIFIC RAILROAD

Richard Billingsley

First published 2019

Amberley Publishing
The Hill, Stroud
Gloucestershire, GL5 4EP

www.amberley-books.com

Copyright © Richard Billingsley, 2019

The right of Richard Billingsley to be identified as the Author of this work has been asserted in accordance with the Copyrights, Designs and Patents Act 1988.

ISBN 978 1 4456 8543 4 (print)
ISBN 978 1 4456 8544 1 (ebook)

All rights reserved. No part of this book may be reprinted or reproduced or utilised in any form or by any electronic, mechanical or other means, now known or hereafter invented, including photocopying and recording, or in any information storage or retrieval system, without the permission in writing from the Publishers.

British Library Cataloguing in Publication Data.
A catalogue record for this book is available from the British Library.

Origination by Amberley Publishing.
Printed in the UK.

Appointed GPSR EU Representative: Easy Access System Europe Oü, 16879218
Address: Mustamäe tee 50, 10621, Tallinn, Estonia
Contact Details: gpsr.requests@easproject.com, +358 40 500 3575

Introduction

One of the giants of the United States railroads, the Union Pacific system can trace its roots back to the 1860s and the construction of the first of the transcontinental railroads across America: the Overland Route.

Construction began at Omaha, Nebraska, in 1862 and a route was forged west with the intention of meeting up with the Central Pacific Railroad, a route started in Sacramento, California, the building of which was heading east at a rapid pace. The two routes came together at a point near Promontory, Utah, and the historically renowned Golden Spike ceremony of 10 May 1869 marked the completion of the first east to west railroad.

This route opened up the west; cross-country journeys that previously took weeks and months to complete became possible in days and the Union Pacific quickly grew to serve thirteen states in the north and west. A period of financial instability in the 1890s stifled growth for a time, but throughout the twentieth century the railroad expanded by construction and by the takeover of smaller systems and individual short lines.

Through mergers with the Missouri Pacific and Western Pacific in the early 1980s and outright acquisition in 1996 of the Southern Pacific Railroad (whose colours are still carried by a number of UP locomotives), the Union Pacific has become the second largest of the Class I railroads with over 32,000 route miles in twenty-three states from the Pacific coast to Illinois, Arkansas and Louisiana and only the BNSF system is larger. In addition, the railroad also has trackage rights on over 1,000 miles of routes belonging to other railroads.

This vast system is powered by a fleet of around 9,000 diesel locomotives, around 100,000 individual freight cars and 50,000 employees. It is entirely a freight operation; the Union Pacific has not operated passenger services since its remaining ones passed to Amtrak, the National Railroad Passenger Corporation, in 1971. The railroad does, however, host many of Amtrak's trains on its tracks, including such famous routes as the California Zephyr, Texas Eagle and Sunset Limited. In the larger metro areas, commuter railroads also make much use of Union Pacific tracks. Amtrak's Pacific Surfliners rely heavily on UP metals, as do the Metrolink services in Southern California. Much of the Chicago commuter area is served by Metra trains on UP track; some of these are also crewed by the railroad.

As well as Amtrak trains, the Union Pacific hosts the freight operations of other Class I railroads on its tracks. A trackage rights system is in place, which allows the railroads to agree to their tracks being used by other railroads' trains where it is strategically necessary. An example of this is the line from Mojave to Bakersfield in California. UP tracks from Los Angeles and the BNSF Railway from Barstow converge in Mojave, a single UP-owned route then heads north-west to Bakersfield, where the two companies' routes split to take different courses to the San Francisco Bay area. Although Union Pacific-owned, over half of the forty or so trains a day that traverse the route are BNSF-operated.

The Union Pacific's locomotive fleet is composed entirely of units from two manufacturers: EMD (Electro-Motive Diesel) and GE (General Electric). GE have supplied more of the recent purchases, but the railroad has large fleets from both companies; the UP particularly favoured the EMD SD60 and SD70 series of locomotive in their various forms and the large SD70ACe model was still being delivered in 2017. In recent years, the railroad has invested heavily in the GE Evolution series of locomotive.

Virtually any locomotive, regardless of manufacturer, can work with another. The long but comparatively light intermodal train may only be hauled by two or three units while a heavy coal or grain train may have as many as ten locomotives in its consist. Distributed power units (DPUs) are common: the ten-locomotive train would typically have five units at the front, three at the rear and two cut into the middle of the train. Control by a telemetry system means that all locomotives are controlled by the crew in the lead locomotive.

The standard locomotive livery for the Union Pacific is yellow with a grey roof, divided by a red line. The red bodyside Union Pacific lettering has given way in recent years to a billowing Stars and Stripes flag with a small UP shield logo. Numbers are in red on the cab side and the locomotive designation is generally underneath in small black lettering. The yellow livery has been in use since the 1930s and is now one of the world's most enduring railroad liveries.

Unlike the UK railway system, the American railroad still has vast amounts of private sidings, serving individual factories and warehouses, and local train workings to serve them. Individual wagons are collected and delivered and sorted into long-distance manifest workings using traditional and hump-style marshalling yards. While currently in a slow decline, this type of working still provides a large income for the railroad and transport for a huge variety of goods.

Alongside this are modern intermodal and piggyback-style trains; one train will often convey in excess of 200 individual containers, many of them double-stacked in well cars. Spine cars carry semi-trailers; these are often worked with intermodal services and are used by companies such as Amazon to move truckloads of deliveries from one hub to another.

Grain, oil products, timber and steel also provide valuable sources of traffic and despite the shift away from coal for power generation, it continues to be moved in huge quantity. Double-decker auto-racks are used to move the car industry's products around; even the US military extensively uses the railroad to move its equipment.

It would obviously be impossible to show every aspect of the Union Pacific Railroad in a single book: trains weave through cities, across deserts and over mountains. I hope the selection included is enough to give the reader a good idea of what they might find should they be planning a visit to the Union Pacific in the western half of the United States.

A Quick Explanation of Locomotive Designations

To the casual viewer or someone interested in trains who has little knowledge of American railroads, the designations used for different types of motive power might seem bewildering. The following notes will help to understand the different types of locomotives.

For much of the past forty years, the market in the US has been dominated by two manufacturers: Electro-Motive Division (EMD) – a General Motors subsidiary until 2005, now owned by Progress Rail – and General Electric (GE).

The larger of the two manufacturers is General Electric; they currently hold two-thirds market share. The current Evolution series started production in 2003 and over 5,000 units have been built. Some of the varying types are detailed below.

ES44DC – Evolution Series, 4,400 hp, DC traction motors
ES44AC – Evolution Series, 4,400 hp, AC traction motors
ES44C4 – Evolution Series, 4,400 hp, AC traction motors, A-1-A trucks with centre unpowered axle
ET44AC – Tier 4 Evolution, 4,400 hp, AC traction motors
ET44C4 – Tier 4 Evolution, 4,400 hp, AC traction motors, A-1-A trucks with centre unpowered axle

A letter H at the end of a designation indicates that the locomotive is a ballasted, heavier version with increased tractive adhesion, e.g. ET44AH instead of ET44AC. A CTE designation denotes use of controlled tractive equipment, similar to Sepex traction motors in the UK, e.g. C45ACCTE. The UK Powerhaul Class 70, PH37ACmi, is loosely based on the Evolution platform.

Many locomotives built before the Evolution series remain in use. These include the Dash-8 and Dash-9 series locomotives, C40-8W (4,000 hp Dash-8) and C44-9W (4,400 hp Dash-9). Both designs use DC traction motors; they were superseded by the AC4400CW (UP designation C45ACCTE) locomotives built with AC motors.

The second manufacturer is Electro-Motive. The company has produced locomotives since the 1930s and became the market leader, overtaking the American Locomotive Company (ALCO) in the 1960s. That dominance was lost to General Electric in the late 1980s, but EMD still produces much equipment for both domestic and international markets.

The GP – general purpose – locomotives are four-axle units built from 1949 to 1994 utilising EMD 567, 645 or 710 series engines. Many GPs have been rebuilt for extended service, and while their days of long-distance, high-speed work are long gone, they are still prolific on local trip workings and yard duty.

The SD – standard duty – locomotives are the larger six-axle units built from 1952 onwards using the EMD 265, 567, 645, 710 and 1010 series engines. The SD40 variant is basically a larger version of the GP locomotive, but the SD series has evolved to produce large, high-powered units such as the SD70ACe, in production since 2003. The Union Pacific was by far the largest customer for the SD70M; they purchased around 1,500 of the 4,000 hp locomotive.

The designations on EMDs differ to those on GE locomotives in that the numbering – SD40, SD60, etc. – refers to SD models rather than engine output. SD units up to the SD60M and SD70M have DC traction motors; the SD60MAC and SD70MAC variants were the first to offer AC equipment. The SD70MAC was replaced in 2003 by the SD70ACe, which is now the standard EMD heavy hauler; its latest guise is the SD70ACe-T4, which complies with Tier 4 emissions legislation.

SD locomotives in current use vary from the 3,000 hp SD40, 3,800 hp SD60 and 4,000 hp SD70M to the 4,300 hp SD70ACe and 6,000 hp SD90MAC.

A southbound mixed train of intermodal stacks and piggyback trailers rounds the tight curve at Warren, a couple of miles to the north of Mojave, CA, on 3 July 2013. The train has been descending for nearly 20 miles from Tehachapi Summit.

Around 10 miles to the north of the previous picture, the Highway 58 intersection with Cameron Road offers a great stopping point to catch northbound trains as they battle with the long climb up to Tehachapi. Three GE Gevo units take the strain as they head north on 16 September 2018.

Barstow, CA, is a major hub for the BNSF Railway, with a large diesel shop and hump classification yard, but the Union Pacific also has tracks through the town. This westbound stack train is waiting alongside the I-40 Interstate freeway to pass through the maze of tracks. Note the third locomotive in the train, hired-in from CSX Transportation. 19 September 2018.

Extra locomotives added to a train to assist with a steep climb are referred to as helpers in the US, and the Utah town of Helper gained its name from the practise. The locomotives here add extra horsepower for the climb to Soldier Summit on the route north to Salt Lake City. C44ACCTE No. 7171 leads a line of four units awaiting duty on 12 September 2018.

A panned shot of a C45ACCTE and an SD70M leading a short train of refrigerated vans (reefers) at Alexander, ID, on 9 September 2018. The GE loco, No. 5599, carries the most recent variation of the UP livery, albeit a rather faded one.

The setting sun illuminates C45ACCTE No. 5910 as it awaits the signal to proceed south at the head of an intermodal at Yermo, CA, on 19 September 2018. Yermo houses a yard and diesel shop for the UP; the facilities are rather more modest than those of the BNSF in nearby Barstow.

Grade crossings are a huge part of the railroad scene in the US; there are over 200,000 in the lower forty-eight states. This is the most basic version: just signs to warn of tracks, no lights, no barriers. 6 October 2015 sees C45ACCTE No. 5740 crossing the road at O'Fallons Junction, NE, leading box hoppers towards the nearby North Platte yard.

DPUs – distributed power units – are not so common on intermodal traffic, although they are by no means rare. This train of boxes heading east from Rock Springs, WY, has a single unit, GE C45ACCTE No. 5518, at the rear to assist with its long consist. The locomotive is unmanned and controlled by a telematics system.

No matter where you are in the States, utility lines crowd the scenery. Sunrise Canyon, CA, is no exception and a train of southbound stacks led by GE Gevo No. 7491 passes under the lines leading to the nearby Cool Water gas power generation plant on 19 September 2018.

A pair of EMD SD40-N locomotives lead a short local trip from Wendover to Salt Lake City through the Hogs Back Pass at Delle, UT, on 5 September 2018. Just off the I-80, the location is close to the south-western corner of the Great Salt Lake.

Late low sun reflects off the Union Pacific 'wings' emblem that adorns the nose of SD70M No. 4942 as it and three more units grind upgrade at Peru Hill, WY, on 9 September 2018.

A pair of EMD SD70ACe locomotives lead two GE Gevo units as they head east near to Colorado City, TX, on 30 October 2017. The locomotives use the two-stroke EMD 710 series engine, rated at 4,300 or 4,500 hp, and each locomotive weighs around 210 tons.

The vast majority of the current UP loco fleet is able to work with any other locomotive; this is demonstrated by GE ES44AC No. 7614 and EMD SD70M No. 4375 as they leave Rock Springs, WY, eastbound on a double-stacked intermodal on 10 September 2018.

A combination of car-carrying auto-racks and stack intermodal boxes rounds towards Daggett, CA, on 18 October 2018 with GE ES44AC No. 7788 leading. At Daggett, the train will use the UP tracks that head east towards Las Vegas and Salt Lake City.

More SD70ACe power leading the way, this time at Ilmon, CA, on 17 October 2018. This manifest train conveys a variety of goods, many of which will be destined for private owner sidings. The US railroad is still heavily involved with traffic that is collected and delivered in individual loads, moved across the country via marshalling yards and mixed traffic trains.

The Lehigh cement works at Monolith, near Tehachapi, CA, is served by a local from Mojave, 20 miles distant. GE C45AH No. 8075 leads a southbound manifest past the works as No. 2430 and another SD60M wait in the siding to follow downgrade. 27 January 2015.

UP power on Eastern Idaho Railroad tracks at Rupert, ID, on 6 September 2018. The Eastern Idaho started operation in 1993, using routes once owned by the UP; however, the yellow locos are still seen in Rupert as they exchange traffic to and from the Eastern Idaho system here. C45ACCTE locomotives are seen either side of an SD70ACe.

BNSF and UP tracks briefly converge to the east of Sweetwater, TX, and run parallel for a half mile or so before taking their own courses. On 31 October 2017, a UP manifest heads west alongside rival trackage with ES44AC No. 7663 being led by ES44AH No. 2527.

Left: With the dynamic brake system squealing, an SD70ACe leads a long double-stack intermodal cautiously down the 1 in 40 incline into Mojave, CA, on 17 September 2018. It will take the full power of both the locomotive dynamic brakes and the train air brake to control the descent into the desert town.

Below: A rich seam of coal and a railroad with the ability to transport that coal brought prosperity to the town of Rock Springs in western Wyoming from the mid-nineteenth century. That prosperity is still remembered in the town today as SD70M No. 4854 leads a classmate east through the downtown area on 10 September 2009.

The two major railroads in the west, the Burlington Northern & Santa Fe Railway and the Union Pacific Railroad, cross each other on the short section of double track at Bealville, CA. Between them, they have over 65,000 route miles of track in the western United States.

A brace of SD70Ms lead a short train of oil tanks west at Castle Rock, WY, on 12 September 2018. The tanks are being returned to service after repair at the works of the Union Tank Car Company in nearby Evanston.

Above: Another EMD loco pairing, this time SD70ACe No. 8830 leading SD70M No. 4249 on a westbound manifest at West Wendover, NV, on 4 February 2015. The 'S' bend the train is traversing affords a good view of the variety of freight cars that can be found in a manifest train.

Below: Unusually powered by a single SD60M, the local from Mojave sits in the cement works sidings at Monolith, CA, on 6 July 2013. No. 2529 will take the loaded cars down to the yard at Mojave for onward movement. C45ACCTE No. 5480 passes southbound as a DPU at the rear of an intermodal.

Sunset at Wendover, UT. Nos 1668 and 1860, both SD40-Ns, had spent the afternoon assembling their train in the small yard and are lined up ready for departure the next morning. The setting sun highlights the train on 4 September 2018.

A pair of SD70M locomotives led by No. 3990 bring a train off the Lone Pine branch and, after the northbound train in the foreground has passed, will head into the yard at Mojave, CA, on 6 March 2015. Despite appearances, there is not about to be a train wreck: there is another running line obscured from view.

Alexander, ID, on 9 September 2018 with C45ACCTE No. 5599 heading east with refrigerated vans. The old Highway 30 leads towards the railroad and from this point parallels the tracks west for many miles.

Led by C45ACCTE units, an eastbound manifest gets into its stride in a golden hour shot taken at Roscoe, TX, on 31 October 2017. The locomotives, Nos 6147 and 6527, will take the train to the Davidson yard at Fort Worth.

27 January 2015 sees a work-stained pair of SD60Ms, Nos 2430 and 2478, at the cement works at Monolith, CA. The works were established in the early twentieth century to provide material for use in constructing the Los Angeles Aqueduct, a system of waterways that take water down from the Sierra Nevada to Los Angeles.

Viewed just off the Lincoln Highway between Lexington and Cozad in Nebraska, SD40-Ns Nos 1587 and 1589 head west with a local that originated from Lincoln, 180 miles to the east. Another UP train is seen following on the adjacent track.

The railroad hosts Amtrak passenger services on some of its routes and has done so since leaving the passenger business in 1971. However, it does not prioritise Amtrak services over its own operation, and lengthy delays can occur. This train, the westbound California Zephyr, is running exactly to time as it sweeps towards the stop at Helper, UT, on 12 September 2018. The following night, the train was over 3 hours late.

The mile-long intermodal. Four locomotives, a couple of hundred boxes and a handful of semi-trailers at Blairtown, WY, on 11 September 2018. The train is led by No. 7510, a GE ES44AC.

The opposite end of the scale. Just six wagons are led by two SD70M locomotives, Nos 4607 and 4372, at Castle Rock, WY, on 12 September 2018. The train was heading for Evanston, just a few miles further east.

6 October 2015 sees C45ACCTE No. 6055 assisting as a distributed power unit at the rear of a long formation of loaded coal wagons. The train is passing O'Fallons Junction, joining the main UP trans-con eastbound, and will eventually arrive at one of the generation plants serving the power-hungry north-eastern United States.

Accidents will happen. On 17 September 2018, a northbound manifest passes the site of a previous mishap near to Tunnel 2 at Caliente, CA. With a 1 in 40 incline, tight reverse curves and a tunnel, guiding a mile-long train in either direction is a task that must require exceptional nerve and skill. Even then, it can still go wrong…

A long redundant crane and caboose watch silently as SD70Ms assemble their train at Evanston, WY, on 11 September 2018. Evanston has an old Union Pacific locomotive roundhouse which is currently being restored as part of the UP railroad complex in the town.

Cresting the summit at Daggett, CA, an ES44AC leads EMD units at the front of a mixed train of auto-racks and intermodal boxes. The last of the four locomotives, No. 9051, is an SD70AH-T4, the latest evolution of the SD series locomotive, designed specifically to meet Tier 4 emissions specifications. 11 September 2018.

The last UP locomotive to carry its original Denver & Rio Grande Western Railroad colours was GP60 No. 1900, seen at Texarkana, a city straddling the border of Texas and Arkansas, on 21 October 2017. The locomotive was new to the DRGW in 1988, the same year the railroad merged with the Southern Pacific, which subsequently merged with the UP in 1996. Regrettably, the locomotive received standard UP yellow paint in April 2018.

Two CSX Transportation-owned GE locomotives stand with a UP ES44AC at Yermo, CA, on 18 September 2018. The Class I railroads frequently hire in power from each other to meet traffic requirements; this results in 'foreign' power appearing at locations far from home – CSX are based in Jacksonville, FL.

It can be hard to appreciate the length of a train just by looking at the front; this view from the rear conveys the sheer scale of railroad operation in America. The 211 containers dwarf the four locomotives in the lead as this train heads east alongside the I-80 Interstate at Rock Springs, WY, on 10 September 2018.

Success can be measured by number, and production of 5,000 locomotives is a sure sign of success. GE Gevo No. 5000 is an ES44AC delivered to the UP in mid-2012 and was seen at Mojave, CA, on 6 October 2015, providing rear-end power to a long train of coal wagons. In September 2017, the number built passed the 10,000 mark.

Having stopped to deliver a few cars into a factory siding, SD70M locomotives Nos 4607 and 4372 reform their train before heading east to Evanston, WY, with their remaining load. The train is seen at Echo, UT, on 12 September 2018.

With around 9,000 locomotives to choose from, it's not often that two consecutively numbered units will be together, but it can happen occasionally. Mojave, CA, on 24 June 2012 saw C45ACCTEs Nos 5409 and 5408 together as they departed south with similar locomotive No. 5545 and box cars.

At Daggett, CA, the UP tracks from Los Angeles and Barstow leave the BNSF trans-con route to head north-east to Las Vegas and Salt Lake City. On 19 September 2018, C45ACCTE No. 6023 turns north across the Santa Fe Street grade crossing with a manifest destined for the UP yard at Yermo, just a couple of miles on.

Dwarfed by the grain elevator that stands lineside, ES44AC No. 7412 leads west from Roscoe, TX, with another double-stacked intermodal on 1 November 2017. Track renewal work was taking place at the time, hence the rather large stack of used ties to the left.

Trackside grain elevators are a prominent feature in the agricultural western states of the US; this one at Scoular, ID, is still served by a private siding. Stabled at the head of a train of empty grain cars on 6 September 2018, C45ACCTE No. 5644 waits for a relief crew to arrive from nearby Pocatello.

Nearby the old railroad town of Bancroft in Idaho's Portneuf Valley, C45ACCTE No. 5599 heads east with a short train of white refrigerated vans on 9 September 2018. As with so many other towns established in the time of railway construction, Bancroft is virtually deserted, and the railroad now passes by almost unnoticed.

Stationed alongside the platform of the Amtrak station at Helper, UT, two sets of locomotives await the call to assist. Northbound trains from Helper face a tortuous 15-mile 1 in 50 climb to Soldier Summit on the old Rio Grande route to Provo and Salt Lake City, and these locomotives are used as required to assist trains up. 12 September 2018.

5 July 2013 sees ES44AC No. 7842 leading two SD70ACe units across the dry creek at Ilmon, CA, with double-stacked well cars. A visit here three months earlier in the year provides a very different view, with greenery on the hills and fast-flowing water in the creek.

The three different types of locomotive on this train demonstrate the ability of nearly all types to work together. SD70AH No. 8838 leads SD70M No. 5000 and C45ACCTE No. 6145 west alongside the Kimama Highway in rural Idaho. Virtually all units use the standard AAR (Association of American Railroads) multiple working equipment.

C45ACCTE No. 5546 guides its eastbound train in towards the yard at Green River, WY, on 11 September 2018. This locomotive is one of a batch of 200 units that were delivered to the railroad in the first half of 2005.

The tall concrete grain elevators at Cozad, NE, provide a backdrop to this eastbound coal train headed by C45ACCTEs Nos 5692 and 5983. Cozad lies on a densely used section of triple track that bisects the state of Nebraska and was seen in the early afternoon of 7 October 2015.

The unmistakable profile of an EMD SD70ACe, in this case No. 8499, leads an intermodal south across Arroyo Avenue in Mojave, CA. The cab window arrangement on the SD70ACe is a new design compared to previous SD locos. 17 September 2018.

The Gevo in profile: ES44AC No. 7970 in charge of two more units and a long train of double-stacks at Glenns Ferry, ID, on 7 September 2018. The cab and body styling have changed little in the fifteen-year history of the design.

Heavy hauling in Texas: ET44AH No. 2685 draws forward into the downtown area of the city of Trent with intermodal boxes heading west. When this photograph was taken on 1 November 2017, the locomotive had only been in service for around a year.

With their armour-yellow colours virtually blending in with the parched hillside, this four-unit manifest rounds into Caliente, CA, on 17 September 2018. The near flat terrain from Bakersfield gives way here to mountains; the climb up to Tehachapi Summit will take more than an hour, often at little more than walking pace.

Leaving by the northern exit, ES44AC No. 7788 heads a mix of stacks and racks away from the yard at Yermo, CA, on 18 September 2018. Heading through the Mojave National Preserve, the next major centre of population the train will encounter will be Las Vegas, NV.

Following the natural curvature of the Snake River, the tracks in the surrounds of King Hill, ID, offer some great views across water and around curves. The westbound manifest in view shows just a fraction of the freight cars in current use, including both small and large box cars, lumber carriers, oil cans and hoppers that may contain a variety of loads. 7 September 2018.

A very unusual sight on the BNSF southern Trans-Con: this double stack intermodal is headed by two UP units sandwiching a CSX locomotive at Cadiz, CA, on 30 January 2017. Union Pacific does not have trackage rights here; the most likely explanation is that the locomotives were on loan to the BNSF Railway.

C45ACCTE No. 6023 leads a Yermo, CA-bound manifest through the long sweeping curve at Nebo, close to Barstow, CA. The fourth locomotive in the train, an AC60CW, carries CSX colours, but is one of a batch of nearly 100 locomotives sold to Progress Rail Leasing. 19 September 2018.

Approaching the yard at Yermo, CA, ES44AC No. 7795 crosses tracks with a relatively short, at least by American standards, train of double-stacks on 19 September 2018. The train was being stabled at Yermo for a time and was crossing tracks to enable entry to the sidings.

A perfect sunny day at Merkel, TX, sees C45ACCTEs sandwiching an SD70M while leading a manifest west through the town on 2 November 2017. The train was travelling slowly at this point; it was about to be overtaken by a faster intermodal service.

A telephoto lens accentuates every lump and bump in the surrounds of Adelaide, ID, on 6 September 2018. With around 13,000 hp on hand, the engineer will hardly have noticed the small summit his train has just crossed.

Along Edison Highway, south of Bakersfield, CA, a four-unit manifest passes Bena Corral on 17 September 2018. This view would have been largely obscured in previous years by a fertilizer factory. Once rail-served, the factory closed in the late 1980s and survived increasing dereliction until demolition in 2015.

Displaced by more modern communication technology, telegraph pole lines still feature widely in the railway scene. Many of these lines have fallen into disrepair, but this example at Crystal, NV, still looks in reasonable shape. C45ACCTE No. 5678 passes at the rear of an intermodal on 15 September 2018.

Nearly new SD70AH No. 8941 leads slightly older C45ACCTE No. 6181 at Monolith, CA, on 3 March 2016. No. 6181 still carries Southern Pacific colours twenty-one years after delivery to the SP, and twenty years since the railroad ceased to exist. The yellow 'patch' cabside covers the old SP number with its new UP identity.

SD70AH No. 8897 works as a mid-train DPU at Adelaide, ID, on 6 September 2018. The practise of having mid-train units seems to have declined in recent years but is still common on the heaviest of trains.

SD40N locomotive No. 1927 switching in the yard at Green River, WY, on 11 September 2018. The orange beacons on the cab roof indicate that the locomotive is fitted with remote control equipment; when the beacons are flashing, this denotes that the locomotive is working in this mode.

Rounding the giant horseshoe curve at Bealville, CA, ES44AC No. 7742 leads a long manifest north on 17 September 2018. The train is in the final stage of its descent from Tehachapi Summit to Bakersfield and the San Joaquin Valley; cars further back in the formation can be seen to the left of No. 7742's cab roof.

An early afternoon survey of the north end of the UP yard at Yermo sees a lull in activity. There's plenty ready to go, but little movement right now. Even the train on the left, headlights blazing, was still in the same spot at sunset. 19 September 2018.

California sunsets can produce some superb 'golden hour' results. The lines east from Barstow, CA, are positioned perfectly to take advantage of a near-cloudless sunset, and on 3 February 2017 SD70AH No. 8894 leads three C45ACCTE units round the curve at Nebo. Timing is everything: the window for this shot is only around twenty minutes.

Past glories on display at the closed Union Pacific station at Shoshone, ID, on 6 September 2018. For many years, the railroad advertised itself as 'The Overland Route'. The station closed in 1991 with the discontinuation of Amtrak's thrice-weekly Pioneer route from Chicago to Seattle.

The fierce climb to Soldier Summit from Helper, UT, involves a couple of tunnels, a fast-flowing river and multiple sharp curves. A northbound manifest enters the Nolan tunnel on 3 February 2015. The SD40N, No. 1653, was in transit and not under power.

Led by an SD70M, a four-unit oil train heading east at Middle Baxter Road, east of Rock Springs, WY. The I-80 Lincoln Highway parallels the rails for some distance east from Rock Springs before they veer sharply southwards to avoid some mountainous terrain. 10 September 2018.

The somewhat unwelcoming platform of the Amtrak station at Texarkana, TX, hosts SD70M No. 5140, leading a four-unit manifest on 20 September 2017. The fifth loco, an SD40N, is another loco in transit, not being used to power the train. In just a few yards, the train will cross the Texas–Arkansas state line.

Dry plains at the summit of Peru Hill, east of Green River, WY, surround a manifest on the westbound track on 11 September 2018. The locomotives, C45ACCTEs No. 5866 and No. 7131, are running as DPUs, powering at the rear of the long formation.

Another DPU helping from the back. C45ACCTE No. 5461 looks as if it hasn't much to do as it rolls downgrade from Siberia, CA, on 30 January 2017, but the dynamic braking power of the locomotive is just as important as its hauling ability. The rails here parallel the historic Route 66 for many miles in either direction.

By American standards, this is not a long train. But it still has a payload of around 140 containers. A trek from the high desert south-west brings ES44AC No. 7795 towards Minneola Road, close to Yermo, CA. The train will continue south to the Los Angeles area, through Barstow and across the Cajon Pass. 19 September 2018.

So many settlements on the old roads have declined since the building of the Interstates bypassed their communities. This abandoned service station in Yermo, CA, was likely a hive of activity fifty years ago, with a forecourt, service bay and parking lot. Then came the I-15. The railroad remains faithful, however, and UP units wait to enter the yard on 19 September 2018.

Unusually, the locomotive fleet available at Mojave, CA, on 20 June 2012 consisted of high horsepower units, including several C45ACCTEs, an SD70ACe and an SD70M. The more usual locomotives stabled at this location would be SD60Ms, used on the local workings to the Lone Pine and Oak Creek branches and the cement works at Monolith.

Snake River reflections near Glenns Ferry, ID, as a westbound intermodal rounds the river's natural curves. Three types of motive power lead: ES44AC No. 7970 is the front unit and SD70M No. 4665 takes the middle, with GEVO Tier 2 prototype No. 5698 on the back. 7 September 2018.

The classic box car, seen in the sidings at Wendover, UT, on 4 September 2018. Many thousands of this type of car have conveyed millions of tons of freight (and quite a count of human cargo too!) across the States for over a century. They might seem a bit of an anachronism in the twenty-first century, but the railroad still heavily relies on them.

The small UP facility at Montpelier, ID, with SD70Ms stabled opposite. Local day-to-day administration of the railroad in the area will be carried out here, including coordination for local workings and maintenance of way work. Taken on a very quiet Sunday 9 September 2018.

Front-end comparison of two EMD locomotives at Texarkana, TX, on 20 September 2018. Both EMD products, GP60 No. 1900 dates from 1988 and was originally owned by the Denver & Rio Grande Western Railroad; SD70M No. 4977 was built in 2002, one of over 1,500 of the type owned by the Union Pacific.

ES44AC No. 7880 heads a trio of locomotives running west at Peru Hill, WY, on 11 September 2018. The train is passing below the I-80 Interstate, a 2,900-mile road from San Francisco to New Jersey which threads through eleven states.

Amid the wires of the Edison substation of the Bakersfield Power Company, SD70ACe No. 8618 leads a classmate and two more units south from the UP Bakersfield facility on 17 September 2018. Heading for Los Angeles, the train faces the long, slow climb to Tehachapi before dropping down to Mojave and Lancaster, through the Cajon Pass and San Bernardino.

8 September 2018 sees ET44AH No. 2586 at McCammon, ID, leading a manifest under the signal bridge. The local area is still controlled by older searchlight signals; these are being replaced nationwide by new three-aspect LED signals.

Just off the I-20 at Blue Flats Road near Gordon, TX, the grade crossing and sweeping curve provide a great opportunity for shots of westbounds, and a break from the monotony of a long drive. ES44AC No. 7719, C45ACCTE No. 6035 and SD70M No. 4657 power through with a long manifest on 2 November 2017.

The main street in the city of Rock Springs, WY, is bisected by the tracks of the Union Pacific railroad. Here, SD70AH-T4C No. 8997 leads a coal train through the town in the midday sun of 10 September 2018. The locomotive is the latest variant in the long history of the SD70, built to satisfy the requirements of Tier 4 emissions regulations.

Way off the beaten track, near to Pebble, ID, a manifest heading for Pocatello turns to the south led by ES44AC No. 2586. All four units on the train carry the latest 'billowing flag' livery, but the paint hasn't worn so well on the second loco, C45ACCTE No. 5811. 8 September 2018.

Drifting slowly west, two DPUs bring the rear of a westbound manifest through Merkel, TX, on 1 November 2017. The two units, C45ACCTE No. 6020 and SD70M No. 4279, date from 2003 and 2000 respectively. Their days as lead units are possibly over, but they have much work of this nature ahead of them.

Pictured amid the clutter of a working rail yard, C45ACCTEs Nos 6064 and 5587 sandwich SD70M No. 4843. The location is the Eastern Idaho Railroad's facility in Rupert, ID. Seen on 7 September 2018, this yard and line were run by the Union Pacific until its sale in 1993.

Another depot scene, this time at Green River, WY. The morning of 11 September 2018 sees ET44AH No. 2563 sharing a rest spot with an unidentified SD70M. The main diesel shop here now maintains the railroad's local fleet of maintenance of way trucks, but servicing and fuelling of locomotives still takes place here.

Led by SD70AH No. 8927, a line of seven locomotives leads an eastbound manifest through the pole lines of Glenns Ferry, ID, on 7 September 2018. Only the front four locomotives were under power; the other three were in transit, either to work in another area or for maintenance purposes.

Leading a train of around 140 grain cars, C45ACCTE No. 5805 clatters over the switches at O'Fallons Junction, near Hershey, NE, on 6 October 2015. Each car weighs around 120 tons loaded; the weight of the train without locomotives is in the region of around 17,000 tons.

C45ACCTE No. 5587 and SD70M No. 4843 at Inkom, ID, on the quiet Saturday afternoon of 8 September 2018. Breaking the silence, the pair were leading the first train in around 2 hours to pass through the town. Sited in the Portneuf Valley, to the south of Pocatello, the area was once part of the large Fort Hall Indian Reservation.

Approaching Merkel, TX, on 2 November 2017, ES44AH No. 8208 and ES44AC No. 7604 lead an intermodal over one of the many farm to market roads that criss-cross this agricultural area of western Texas.

Idaho Falls, ID, is the location for this lazy Saturday evening shot of a pair of SD40Ns at rest. No. 1649 dates from early 1980, No. 1846 from the summer of 1973. Both units were new to the Union Pacific and have been rebuilt at the company's Jenks Shop at North Little Rock, AR. 8 September 2018.

Passing the grain elevators at Talmage Road, Bancroft, ID, this train of reefers is making steady progress east on 9 September 2018. Reefer vans are used to convey fresh, chilled products; one of the main commodities carried by this means is oranges and orange juice.

The most basic of grade crossings employ just a stop sign and warning and emergency contact notices. This private crossing at Warren, CA, had notice of intended closure by the railroad posted at the time this picture was composed, 30 June 2013. C45ACCTE No. 5376 leads a train composed mainly of auto-racks north.

Coal on the move through Oshkosh, NE, on 5 October 2015. Nos 6596 and 6452 are both C45ACCTEs, dating from 2000 and 1996 respectively. The train will likely have a crew change at the UP's large hub at North Platte, NE, around 2 hours further on.

After a brief stop to allow a train to clear the single-track section in front, C45ACCTE No. 5597 leads SD70M No. 5163 and ES44AC No. 7449 away from the junction with the Eastern Idaho Railroad at Minidoka, ID, on 6 September 2018. The white reefer vans are sadly particularly prone to graffiti attacks.

The sun sets over the distant city of Bakersfield on 11 April 2014. This is Sandcut, 10 miles south on the UP line to Mojave. A line block up ahead sees trains being stacked while the tracks are cleared: ES44AC No. 7951 leads two more units on a short hopper train; immediately behind is a train of double stacks and in the distance a bright light indicates the presence of another train.

The small settlement of Caliente, CA, is where the climb to Tehachapi Summit starts, or where the descent ends. With a BNSF train in the final stage of its descent in the background, SD70ACe No. 8618 waits for its turn on the single track ahead. 17 September 2018.

With the notorious I-15 interstate in the distance, ES44AC No. 7491 approaches Minneola Road with stacks from the north on 19 September 2018. A drive of around 3 miles along Minneola Road in an eastbound direction from here will take you to the grade crossing on the BNSF Trans-Con and Route 66.

SD70ACe No. 8510 brings up the rear of a southbound train of auto-racks at Bealville, CA, on 23 June 2012. As the racks are lightweight in comparison to some other types of traffic, it's not so common to find a DPU on a train of this type; trains of around 100 loaded vehicles are often handled by just two locomotives.

SD70Ms in profile at Evanston, WY, on 11 September 2018. The earlier unit, No. 3858, dates from 2001 while No. 5141 was among the last of the type to be delivered to the Union Pacific in late 2004.

As dusk begins to fall, the floodlights at Green River, WY, will soon be illuminating some night-time activity. SD40N No. 1927 reforms a westbound train while its two SD70M locomotives had been taken for refuelling. 9 September 2018.

A trio of Gevo locomotives accelerate south at Ilmon, CA, on 1 March 2016. Leading ES44AH No. 8196 is around eighteen months old, but the tailing ET44AT locomotives, Nos 2582 and 2615, had only been in service for a few weeks; both were delivered to the railroad at the end of 2015.

The world-famous Tehachapi loop lies on the UP tracks from Bakersfield to Mojave, CA, and is part of the ascent from the near sea level southern San Joaquin Valley to Tehachapi, the summit lying at around 4,000 feet. Long trains will cross over or under themselves as they negotiate the loop's spiral, which elevates the track by around 80 feet. 22 June 2012.

Rising in Wyoming, the Snake River passes through Idaho on its 1,100-mile course to the Columbia River and eventually the Pacific Ocean. Railroad and river meet frequently and the pleasant community at King Hill, ID, is an ideal location to watch the trains go by. A westbound intermodal drifts by on the warm afternoon of 7 September 2018.

GP38-2 No. 643 at Bakersfield, CA, with a caboose seconded for police use. The diesel facility here has been closed since this picture was taken on 31 March 2014 and the locomotives are gone; the caboose was dumped near to the former fuelling line in late 2018, apparently no longer used.

ES44AC No. 7361 leading a manifest under a sultry Idaho sky on 9 September 2018. Many of the routes across the continent are single-track and passing sidings are frequent, enabling the traffic to keep moving; this train crossed another just a couple of miles further on.

The small yard at Caliente, NV, plays host to C45ACCTE No. 6512 on 3 September 2018. Caliente lies on the tracks from Las Vegas to Salt Lake City; sadly, a lull in traffic here saw no passing trains for several hours, until long after nightfall.

Right: The competing modes of transportation at Peru Hill, WY, on 10 September 2018. Union Pacific stacks led by C45ACCTE No. 5652 are about to change tracks while a flatbed semi-trailer passes overhead on the eastbound I-80 Interstate.

Below: No. 8387, an SD70ACe from 2005, leads a train across the tracks of the Kansas City Southern Railroad and the tarmac of the main Quitman Street in Pittsburg, TX. Despite the warning signs, queueing traffic on the road blocked the rails long after the barriers dropped; one car driver in particular looked increasingly apprehensive as the train drew ever closer.

Led by C45ACCTE No. 5847, an almost uniform train of double-stacked well cars winds past the United States Marine Corps depot at Nebo, CA, on 19 September 2018. The US military has several facilities in the western Mojave Desert area and is an important customer for the railroads.

Another feature of the western Mojave is wind turbines. The area is renowned for its hot but often windy conditions and there are many hundreds of turbines in the 20-mile stretch between Mojave and Tehachapi alone. ES44AC No. 7490 drags an intermodal up towards Tehachapi Summit on 15 September 2018.

The hillsides around Caliente, CA, show the effects of a long, hot summer; the green of March and April has been baked dry by late June. Quadruple SD70Ms lead an intermodal towards Tunnel 2 on 23 June 2012, around five or six months before any significant rainfall can be expected.

A train of repaired tank cars from the Union Tank Car Company winds through Echo Canyon, UT, on 12 September 2018, en route from Evanston, WY, to Ogden, UT. The railroad shares space with the I-80 Lincoln Highway through Echo Canyon.

A close-up view of the business end of SD60M No. 2410 at Yermo, CA, on 19 September 2018. Built in 1990, the locomotive will now be employed on local trip workings – less glamorous than a long intermodal, but absolutely vital to the business of running a railroad.

Three C45ACCTEs, Nos 5596, 5723 and 6013, lead a manifest alongside the Old Oregon Trail Road, close to Lava Hot Springs, ID. The Union Pacific uses its own classification of C45ACCTE on many of its fleet, rather than the official AC4400CW used by General Electric. 9 September 2018.

As noted earlier, the US military uses the railroad to move equipment between bases as needed. This train, led by SD70M No. 4805 and C44ACCTE No. 5649, consists largely of tanks and was captured passing through Hershey, NE, on 6 October 2015.

Now closed, the Union Pacific locomotive depot at Bakersfield, CA, had a turntable in the storage sidings. On 2 July 2013, three locomotives were around the turntable: SD70ACe No. 8361 and two ES44ACs, No. 7763 and No. 7510.

Seen earlier in its journey in a previous picture, SD70AH No. 8927 leads the seven locomotives and the mile-long train along the Snake River at King Hill, ID, on 7 September 2018. Note how the armour-yellow paint used by the UP fares better on some locomotives than others: the third locomotive, ES44AC No. 8112, is only four years old, the same age as the clean-looking SD70AH No. 8906 behind it.

The last rays of the day bathe Rosamund, CA, in warm yellow light as C45ACCTE No. 5464 leads three units and a manifest heading north. The line of the San Andreas Fault, cause of many California earthquakes, lies across the foot of the mountains in the distance. 9 April 2014.

Alongside South Blaser Highway, the old Highway 30, ES44AC No. 7687, with a classmate and a pair of SD70Ms, brings a train of intermodal boxes and piggyback semi-trailers into Lava Hot Springs, ID, on 8 September 2018. The bypassing of this road by a new shorter route has left little traffic on the road, making railroad photography along here much easier!

A snowy scene at Soldier Summit, UT, on 3 February 2015. The five SD70Ms have just brought the train up unaided from Helper and will now go down the other side of the mountain to Provo and Salt Lake City. Summer days here can see temperatures up in the thirties on the centigrade scale; in the winter, the thirties in Fahrenheit is a warm day.

Three of the most recent locomotives on important intermodal work at Bealville, CA, on 1 March 2016. C45AH No. 8196 from 2014 leads two ET44AHs, Nos 2582 and 2613, both of which had only been in service for around four months.

A dust track at Helper, UT, that serves as a car park, an entrance to the yard and part of the Amtrak station platform. A rather weary-looking C45ACCTE from 1999, No. 7171, along with older classmate No. 6607, rests in between duties on 12 September 2018.

Accessed by an old Denver & Rio Grande Western branch from Colton, UT, Skyline Mine at Schofield is served by the Union Pacific. On 13 September 2018, the loading of a train was already in progress so this second train was required to wait until space was available for it at the mine. ES44AC No. 7775 and C45ACCTE No. 6589 are DPUs at the rear.

At around a year old, ES44AC No. 7955 looks smart on the rear of intermodal boxes at Keene, CA. The location lies approximately midway between Edison and Tehachapi, at the foot of the Tehachapi loop, and the frequently alternating single and double track often leads to trains being stacked in one direction while those travelling in the opposite direction pass through. 7 July 2013.

The generous spacing and wide-open nature of much of small-town America is apparent in this shot taken in Shoshone, ID, with SD70AH No. 8865 leading three SD70Ms as they rattle past the site of the one-time passenger station heading west on 6 September 2018.

An encampment during the time of railroad construction, the ghost town of Wahsatch, UT, was abandoned in the 1930s, it's growth stunted by the development of Evanston, just over the border in Wyoming. Nothing now remains other than a few agricultural buildings and a name on the map. 12 September 2018.

A mixed bag of motive power enters Mojave, CA, under the Highway 14 bridge at the south end of the town. Highway 14 largely parallels the railroad to the northern end of Lancaster, around 20 miles distant, at which point the tracks head south-east to Los Angeles via the Cajon Pass, while the highway takes the more direct route south through the Antelope Valley. 24 June 2012.

The cantilever at Sandcut, CA, was a popular feature with photographers, along with a similar structure at Tehachapi depot; the two were the last of their type on the Mojave sub. The one at Tehachapi was taken down in April 2013 while this one was gone by February 2014. New signals lie in wait nearby on 2 July 2013 as a train of bare tables passes by.

Switching at Yermo, CA, on 18 September 2018. SD70M No. 4440 and ex-Southern Pacific C45ACCTE No. 6187 are busy assembling a train which they would later take north to Las Vegas.

At the west end of Glenns Ferry, the I-84 Interstate and the railroad converge to pass through the Snake River valley. The interstate is carried on two levels by a massive concrete bank while the railroad takes a lower course alongside the old Highway 30. A westbound manifest takes the corner on 7 September 2018.

Less heavy than trains of grain or oil, intermodals will often need only two or three locomotives. This train, headed by SD70ACe No. 8802 and an older SD70M, has coped fine with the gradients as it approaches Tehachapi Summit from Mojave on 30 March 2014. The rear of the train can just be seen in the far-right distance.

The Union Pacific retains a fleet of around forty-five passenger cars that are used for its business train. The cars are well over half a century old now but can be seen from time to time out on the network. On 6 September 2018, the train was out in Idaho and caught at Bannock on its way to the Nampa/Boise area. Formerly SD70AH No. 9026, now No. 1943, the locomotive wears a special 'Spirit of the Union Pacific' livery.

With locomotives from three different railroads at the helm, it's hard to be sure who the operator of this train of military hardware is. The location is the yard at Yermo, CA, which suggests it is UP-operated, the stabled train using a BNSF ES44C4, a UP C44/60AC and an ES40DC from CSX. 18 September 2018.

Mentioned earlier, the fuel rack at Green River, WY, is visited by SD70Ms Nos 4767 and 4854 while their train was being reformed by SD40N No. 1927 in the yard. 9 September 2018.

With the train on the right stopped for a crew break, the advantages of continuous bi-directional signalling are apparent as another train uses the other track to pass on the eastern side of Glenns Ferry, ID, on 7 September 2018. Most of the main routes across the continent are equipped for this to take place.

Stabled in the small yard at Mojave, CA, on 31 March 2014, SD70ACe No. 8336 sits with two GE locomotives at the head of a relatively short train. The facilities at Mojave are intensively used for local traffic to Lancaster, Monolith, Oak Creek and the Lone Pine branch.

The giant EMD DDA40X locomotive. Known as Centennials, forty-seven of these were built for the UP from 1969. Two 645 series engines with a 6,600 hp output powered these 98-foot-long locos, the last of which were retired in 1985. The UP has one in its heritage fleet for occasional use, while this one, No. 6901, was presented to the city of Pocatello, ID, by the railroad.

The line north out of Mojave, CA, is notable for its long, hard climb for loaded trains; by the time they reach Warren, 3 miles distant, they are often down to little more than walking pace. A five-unit GE loco line-up led by ES44AC No. 8032 gets to grips with the adverse gradient on 31 March 2014.

Signal bridges equipped with searchlight-type signals are increasingly becoming a thing of the past as modern three-aspect signalling takes over. This five-signal bridge controls westbound movements from Glenns Ferry, ID, and was still in use on 7 September 2018.

To celebrate the 2002 Winter Olympic Games in Salt Lake City, the railroad turned out two SD70M locomotives in a special blue livery and they were used for the Olympic torch relay across the country. No. 2002 is seen at Mojave, CA, on 27 January 2015. Both locomotives still carry the livery in late 2018.

With less than a year's service on the clock, C45AH No. 8103 rounds the curve towards Tunnel 2 above Caliente, CA, on 8 April 2014, leading an intermodal train south. The landscape is still relatively green; within a few weeks the summer heat will change that.

An SD70M, an SD70MAC and an SD70ACe at Ilmon, CA, with a maintenance of way train on 11 February 2015. The second locomotive, No. 4790 from the CSX Transportation fleet, is the later version with AC traction motors; the UP loco at the front, No. 5028, has the more traditional DC motors.

30 March 2014 sees ES44AC No. 7402 at Monolith heading into the California sunset. Monolith lies 4 miles to the east of Tehachapi, at an elevation of just under 4,000 feet; the area to the right of the train is a dry lake.

The Utah sandstone at Helper, UT, provides a contrast with the yellow of the Union Pacific locomotives and the blue skies of a perfect late summer day. The differing yellows on the three locomotives and subtle differences in the livery can be seen in this profile shot from 12 September 2018.

The country elevator of the Scoular company dominates the scene at Bancroft on 9 September 2018 as ES44AC No. 7381 runs past at the head of a westbound manifest. Bancroft is a small town of less than 400 inhabitants at an elevation of around 5,400 feet; it lies on the old Highway 30 in the south-eastern corner of Idaho.

Older motive power on a high priority intermodal at Eric, CA, on 30 June 2013: C45ACCTE No. 5397 leads two SD70Ms around the wide curve from Monolith. While not unknown on this type of working, these units would usually be found being led by newer GE Gevo or SD70AH locomotives.

A more typical locomotive formation on an intermodal is seen climbing towards Bealville, CA, on 2 July 2013, with ES44AC No. 7846 leading SD70M No. 4206 and C45ACCTE No. 5779. The railroad generally uses newer equipment as the lead locomotive where possible.

Locomotives are regularly loaned between railroads to cater for peak traffic requirements but there is also a healthy locomotive leasing business, with companies buying redundant assets from railroads and leasing to other users. This UP train at Daggett, CA, has ex-CSX Transportation AC60CW No. 627 in its formation on 19 September 2018. The locomotive is now owned by Progress Rail.

Sunset at Yermo, CA, as a SD70M and SD60M combination run in from the north with a train of auto-racks on 19 September 2018. Sadly, there's no such thing as a long summer night in California: at best darkness falls by 7.30 p.m.

6,500 feet up in the Continental Divide, just two locomotives suffice for this westbound intermodal negotiating the triangle of tracks at Point of Rocks, WY, on 10 September 2018. The triangle here provides access from the main east to west route to the Jim Bridger power plant and Black Butte mine.

The Skyline coal mine near Schofield, UT, opened in 1982 and was convenient for the Denver & Rio Grande Scofield branch. The Union Pacific serves the mine today and this train photographed on 13 September 2018 was awaiting clearance to enter the loading area.

Engaging in a little switching, SD40N locomotives Nos 1860 and 1668 put their train together at Wendover, UT, on 4 September 2018. The work concluded a short while later; the locomotives were parked up in readiness for a trip to Salt Lake City the next morning.

No. 5097, one of the later series SD70Ms built in late 2002, hangs onto the rear of a long train of auto-racks as it negotiates the junction at McCammon, ID, on 9 September 2018. Tracks from Brigham City, UT, and Green River, WY, converge at this point and continue north to Pocatello.

After a lunchtime lull in traffic, a southbound manifest breaks the silence at Sandcut, CA, on 17 September 2018. SD70ACes Nos 8618 and 8531 from the 2007 batch of locomotives lead the train, with ES44AC No. 8008 and SD70M No. 4739 behind.

An evening locomotive movement from Helper, UT, to Grand Junction, CO, passes Wellington, UT, on 13 September 2018. The dark cloud above the hills was smoke from a wildfire caused by lightning at Pole Creek, near Provo, UT, around 75 miles distant.

C45ACCTE No. 5564 rounds the curves at Keene, CA, as it descends from the Tehachapi loop to Bakersfield on 29 June 2013. A stationary train of intermodal boxes waits to continue forward on the other track; delays occur frequently in the area as there is a mix of double- and single-track sections for trains to negotiate.

Former UP SD40-2 locomotives Nos 3403 and 3698 are now Nos 720 and 703 in the fleet of the Florida East Coast Railroad. Seen at Cocoa, FL, on 20 January 2012, the pair still wear their yellow and grey UP colours, with the decals of their new owner replacing those of the UP.

A long train of auto-racks is led into Yermo yard by SD70M No. 4476 and SD60M No. 2410 on 19 September 2018. The car carriers are used extensively throughout the country by all the Class I railroads; even Amtrak has a fleet that are used on the Auto-train, a car and passenger-carrying service from Lorton, VA, to Sanford, FL.

Heading for Waycross yard, a CSX train passes over the small summit at Folkston, GA, on 23 January 2012. The third locomotive is Union Pacific SD70M No. 4249, far from home working along the eastern seaboard of the States.

A triple bill of GE locomotives working nose to tail 'elephant' style at Monolith, CA. ES44ACs Nos 7490 and 7891 sandwich C45ACCTE No. 5279 as they head north with an intermodal for the Bay Area on 17 September 2018.

The BNSF Railway on the Union Pacific Railroad. ES44DC No. 7353 is at the head of a train that will use the rival company's tracks for 60 torturous miles before regaining BNSF metals at Kern Junction, to the south of Bakersfield. Pictured at Arroyo Avenue, on the long climb out of Mojave, CA, on 21 June 2012.

ES44AC No. 7896 leads four SD70M locomotives at Glenns Ferry, ID, on 7 September 2018. A typical intermodal train will only need two or three locomotives as they are not generally heavy trains; it is likely that the rear two locomotives are not under power.

GP38-2 No. 280 at Bakersfield, CA, on 23 June 2012, before closure of the diesel sidings. No. 280 was new to the Missouri Pacific in January 1980 as No. 2166, a number retained when the locomotive passed to the UP when the railroads merged in late 1982. The change to No. 280 occurred in 2007 during a large fleet re-numbering.

Switching operations in progress at Mojave, CA, on 1 July 2013. Only one of the eight SD60Ms was under power, lead locomotive No. 2356, but the single wagon at the rear was moved with the entire locomotive consist; trains for local workings to Trona and Monolith were being formed up.

The first of two pictures showing the progress of a long train of auto-racks exiting the Tehachapi loop at Walong, CA. Two Union Pacific locomotives head the 100-rack-long train as it continues the climb to the summit. 24 June 2012.

A couple of minutes later and two-thirds of the train length can be seen as it snakes around the slopes. Construction of the loop and line by the Southern Pacific Railroad was completed by 1876; the line became Union Pacific property in 1996 after acquisition of the Southern Pacific.

Framed by the concrete viaduct carrying State Route 376, a manifest starts out eastbound from Rock Springs, WY, on 10 September 2018 with two SD70Ms leading an ES44AC. The road is a relatively recent construction which links the east side of town to the I-80 Interstate.

C44ACCTE No. 5597 moves slowly over a private grade crossing at Norland, ID. Sadly, the 215,000 grade crossings on America's railroad system suffer an accident approximately every 3 hours; the majority were caused by drivers trying to beat the train or by stalled vehicles. In 2015 over 230 fatalities were recorded.

Patched ex-Southern Pacific C44AC No. 6380 stands with C45ACCTE No. 7122 at Silver Queen Road, to the south of Mojave, CA, with a coal train on 25 June 2012. At the time, well over 200 locomotives still carried SP colours, sixteen years after the company was taken over. Just a handful remain in late 2018.

Although the Tehachapi Mountains can see snow from November to April, the main concentration is likely to be in January or February. On 2 April 2014, a late dusting coats the hills as C45ACCTE No. 5462 battles both gravity and climate with a northbound manifest.